Introdução de Riscos Químicos Emergentes de Nano Partículas

Introdução de Riscos Químicos Emergentes de Nano Partículas

Livro dedicado ao leitor.

Não se encontra ao abrigo do acordo ortográfico de 2014, antes no de 1990 e quiçá antecessores.

ISBN: 9781980828242

Agradecimentos

Mais são os agradecimentos, do que os protestos, ou assim deveria de ser, sou afortunado, quer no muito, quer no pouco, de estar vivo e ter a capacidade de escrever.

Agradeço primeiramente a Deus, pela vida que me dá, onde posso apreciar desde coisas simples a coisas mais elaboradas. Em segundo lugar, não menos importante, ao meu pai, que me tem sido sempre presente e dado de si, sempre pela minha pessoa. Em terceiro lugar, àquelas pessoas, que poucas são, a quem posso considerar de Amigo, neste caso Amigas, sou-vos grato.

Em quarto lugar, e não menos importante, a vós os possíveis leitores, vos agrade este livro de estudo.

Resumo

O presente livro tem como objectivo principal explicar o que são nano partículas, por sua vez exemplificar alguns casos em concreto onde são colocadas em prática, dar alguns casos de riscos emergentes e por fim dar exemplos de prevenção desses mesmos riscos. A opção pelo tema justifica-se por ser algo ainda numa fase emergente/embrionária, havendo ainda poucos estudos abordados, podendo assim abordar um tema inovador e eventualmente facilitar a compreensão a qualquer leitor, este tema ainda pouco estudado.

Palavras-Chave: Nano Partículas, Riscos

Abstract

This book aims to explain what are the nanoparticles, to exemplify some cases in concrete where they are put in practice, to give some examples of risks and finally to give examples of preventing those risks. The choice of this theme is justified because it is something in an emerging/embryonic stage, there are still few published studies, thus being an innovative theme and eventually facilitate the understanding to any reader, about this subject little studied.

Keywords: Nanoparticles, Risks

Índice

Introdução

Este livro foi desenvolvido com o âmbito de poder demonstrar a qualquer leitor o que é de facto uma Nano Partícula, assim como a Nano Tecnologia, analisando assim primeiramente o que são nano partículas, por sua vez analisar o porquê de ser um risco emergente em termos químicos, como avaliar esses riscos, por fim encontrar estratégias para os prevenir. O primeiro capítulo será com base na revisão da literatura, referindo os principais autores que estudaram as nano partículas. No segundo capítulo explicar o que são nano partículas, por sua vez a forma de como se devem avaliar os riscos de nano partículas, bem como o porquê de ser um risco emergente. No terceiro capítulo serão colocadas formas de prevenção destes riscos emergentes químicos de nano partículas.

1. Revisão da Literatura

As nano partículas começaram a ser abordadas de forma mais interessada, há cerca de 10 anos atrás até aos dias de hoje (2016), outrora não havia conhecimento de tais partículas, mas desde o seu descobrimento, que tem sido uma área a emergir, cada vez mais. São apenas visíveis a microscópio e com uma dimensão inferior a 100 nanómetros (de acordo com o Priberam Dicionário), por exemplo 1 milímetro representa 1,000.000 nanómetros. Não existe ainda um consenso sobre uma definição, nem do primeiro autor a descobrir, sendo as dimensões acima referidas, as mais consensuais e aceites. Em anexos (Figura 3 e Figura 4), estão dois exemplos de nano partículas, retirados a microscópio. Para além de ser uma partícula de pequena dimensão, ela transporta propriedades, sendo classificada e diferenciada entre ela, pelo seu diâmetro, as partículas finas têm um intervalo entre 100 e 2500 nanómetros, já as partículas ultrafinas, têm um tamanho entre 1 e 100 nanómetros.

Em si as nano partículas podem ser consideradas moléculas hidrofílidas num espaço interno de lipossomas (sistemas formados por pequenas vesículas fechadas, esféricas e compostas por uma ou mais bicamada de fosfolípidos), podendo ser aquecidas, evaporadas, pressionadas, diluídas, absorvidas, trabalhadas e geneticamente alteradas. As nano partículas existem numa grande variedade de metais, como por exemplo o ouro, cobre, prata e o ruténio. Exemplificando com a nano partícula de ouro (GNPs), esta pode não ser semelhante a um anel de ouro, como o conhecemos, podem antes ser vermelhas e mesmo violetas, depende do seu tamanho e da sua forma, esse processo ocorre nos metais condutores e onde vão ser confinados os movimentos dos electrões que se situam à superfície dos átomos do metal, como da interacção destes com a luz incidente.

As nano partículas, são cada vez mais utilizadas para efeitos de nanotecnologia, seja na área de investigação, desenvolvimento e produção, inovação, industrial, bem como na área da medicina, sendo esta última a que contém mais estudos já realizados, embora com poucos estudos de caso, onde realmente reflictam valores importantes para algum tipo de cura ou prevenção, não obstante dos avanços já alcançados na área científica e de pesquisa, no tocante de combate ao câncer e outras doenças semelhantes, pelos avanços da nanotecnologia.

2. O Que São Nano Partículas?

As nano partículas existem numa grande variedade de metais, como por exemplo o ouro, cobre, prata, ruténio, entre outros, embora qualquer uma das variedades, deve ser protegida, de outra forma irá aumentar o seu tamanho e precipitar, tornando a sua vida útil pequena, para evitar que tal aconteça, utiliza-se um método chamado de estabilização. A imagem da Figura 1, pode ilustrar de uma forma simples, o tamanho de uma nano partícula e como ela fica, caso não tenha esse processo de estabilização.

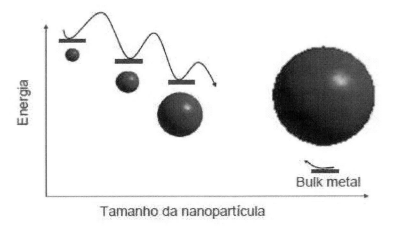

Figura 1- Imagem ilustrativa, de uma nano particula, não estabilizada

Um exemplo do tamanho de uma nano partícula, está por exemplo na dimensão de um cabelo humano que tem de largura cerca de 80,000 nanómetros, por outras palavras 1 Milímetro (mm) representa 1,000.000 Nanómetros (nm).

Outro exemplo ilustrativo da dimensão de nano
partículas:

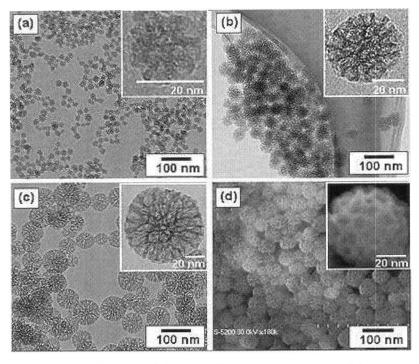

Figura 2- Imagem de ilustração de quão pequenas são as células

(a,b e c) imagens de meso poros preparados de nano partículas de
sílica com diâmetro externo de: (a) 20 nm, (b) 45 nm e (c) 80
nm.

14

2.1 Exemplos de Nano Tecnologia

A nanotecnologia, continua a ser algo em constante inovação, visto que é algo recente e ainda pouco abordado, como estudado. No entanto, já existem várias formas de nanotecnologia, sendo estas algumas delas, de acordo com a Agência Europeia de Segurança e Saúde do Trabalho:

- Chips com nano-electrões, para acelerar a velocidade de computação, de um computador;
- Aplicações biomédicas (implantes, próteses, medicina ultra eficiente, detectores, etc);
- Tecnologia ambiental (selecção de filtros de várias partículas e membranas)
- Tecnologia para energia (como painéis solares, baterias, etc);
- Nos transportes, como eles de aviação ou de transportes espaciais;
- Na agricultura e nutrição (sensores, indicadores de frescura, crescimento, etc);
- Aplicações médicas;
- Cosméticos;
- Tecnologia militar.

2.2 Riscos de Nano Partículas

Cada vez mais existem estudos que demonstram possíveis riscos de que as nano partículas, pode afectar o corpo humano. Não se sabe ainda determinar a extensão desses mesmos danos, no entanto as indicações é que num futuro próximo, quem está em contacto com nano partículas (sejam elas de qualquer tipo e escala), podem contrair efeitos cardiopulmonares, alterações na estrutura proteica, efeitos na auto-imunidade, criação de 'stress' oxidativo e mesmo cancro.

Visto a nanotecnologia e industrial, ser algo relativamente novo e pouco estudado, é difícil prever ou verificar o número de trabalhadores que possam já estar afectos à exposição dos potenciais riscos de nano partículas. De acordo com o relatório da Agência Europeia de Segurança e Saúde do Trabalho, apenas um inquérito de estimativa nas empresas e organizações que utilizam nanotecnologia, seriam um total de 24,388 pessoas, isto em 2004, o que comprova ainda um baixo nível de abordagem à área e preocupação por parte das organizações, de salvaguardar ou prevenir que tais riscos possam acontecer. E com esta carência e despreocupação por parte das organizações, de quererem salvaguardar os interesses dos seus

16

trabalhadores, como da sua segurança e saúde, torna- se mais complicado de prevenir um trabalhador de contrair qualquer tipo de doença ou mal-estar, devido às nano partículas, que possam estar afectas ou vir a afectar o corpo e respectivas células.

O espectável é que a nanotecnologia, cada vez mais cresça a nível global, o que se não for controlável nem houver nenhum método de prevenção, ou ferramentas de prevenção, poderá ser uma futura debilidade a nível organizacional que trabalhe com nano partículas ou nano reagentes, como para os próprios trabalhadores.

Segundo o mesmo relatório feito por parte da Agência Europeia de Segurança e Saúde do Trabalho, há 4 tipos de maior possibilidade de riscos e exposição a riscos, sendo eles:

- Trabalhadores que estejam em contacto com nano materiais em líquido, sem protecções adequadas (por exemplo luvas), o que acresce ao risco de estarem a nível da pele, expostos;

- Trabalhadores que estejam em contacto com nano materiais em líquido, durante o processo de misturas ou tornar em pó, onde haja grande possibilidade de agitação, o que poderá afectar a respiração;

- Trabalhadores que estejam expostos aos gases libertados, em locais não fechados devidamente ou selados, o que cria uma maior probabilidade de aerossol libertado no espaço de trabalho;

- Trabalhadores que tenham contacto directo com pós de nano partículas, terão maior probabilidade de aerossolização.

Com isto previsto, existem maiores probabilidades de problemas cardíacos, de pele, entre outros factores, que podem ser prevenidos atempadamente, antes de agravar a situação dos trabalhadores, como da atmosfera. Os sectores que certamente serão mais afectados de acordo com o mesmo relatório realizado por parte da Agência Europeia de Segurança e Saúde do Trabalho, são:

- Empresas/organizações do sector primário de pesquisa e desenvolvimento (Universidades e outros locais de pesquisa);
- Empresas/organizações que trabalhem mais com pó, processos de pinturas, de pigmentação, cimentos;
- Empresas/organizações de soldagem;
- Empresas/organizações com processos de produção de nano partículas.

Para este tipo de empresa/organização, já deviam estar previstas metodologias de prevenção implementadas e em vigor, o que de momento ainda não acontece ou está numa fase de 'despreocupação', pode ser ainda um risco emergente, no entanto é preferível prevenir do que permitir que se torne um perigo.

Em anexo ficaram pequenos excertos de um texto retirado numa notícia realizada pela RTP, sobre um estudo feito por Peter Dobson, do King's College de Londres, sobre as nano partículas que poluem a atmosfera, terem sido encontradas no cérebro humano, provocando a contribuição do desenvolvimento de doenças neuro degenerativas, como o Alzheimer, resumindo um pouco essa notícia/artigo, o autor chegou à conclusão de que as nano partículas podem penetrar o cérebro humano, representando um risco para a saúde tanto de um trabalhador como de um ser humano alheio a trabalhos que exerçam qualquer tipo de função envolvendo nano partículas, isto através da queima de combustíveis, embora não seja algo ainda com grandes provas científicas, não deixa de ser algo alarmante e que poderia ser prevenido devidamente.

2.3 Alguns dos Dilemas das Nano Partículas

A própria dimensão das particulas, podem ser um problema, porque é sempre necessário material para poder medir tal tamanho ínfimo. Assim como nem sempre se ter o material necessário para poder utilizar as NanoPartículas.

Outro dos dilemas enfrentados é a falta de regulação da nanotecnologia, tanto comercial, como a nível de saúde, embora já existam organizações mundiais de saúde, em si, ainda não passaram das possíveis previsões.

Em si algumas NanoPartículas, tanto podem beneficiar o ser humano, como podem danificar o ser humano, como por exemplo nano partículas de prata, actuam como germicidas em aparelhos como o ar-condicionado, em si matam microorganismos benéficos para o ciclo da vida.

E outro dilema, eventualmente mais grave, é que com o avanço da nanotecnologia, também surgem novas armas, que causam a morte.

3. Formas de Prevenção

Existem já várias formas de prevenção de potenciais riscos emergentes de nano partículas afectarem os trabalhadores e/ou trabalhos que envolvam nano partículas, algumas das formas existentes passam por simples processos de selar equipamentos, outros por usar materiais protectores, como por simples processos de utilizar luvas protectoras, como também podemos verificar que existem formas onde as nano partículas previnem outros fenómenos. Exemplificando melhor a utilização de nano partículas, como forma de protecção, na área dos pesticidas, foi desenvolvido um fato de protecção para a aplicação de pesticidas, feito com base em nano partículas, reutilizável, segundo as boas práticas e requisitos da segurança de trabalho e aplicação do produto, com este pequeno exemplo podemos verificar que existem já formas de prevenção utilizando as nano partículas (informação retirada do artigo da RTP - Portugueses desenvolvem fato de protecção para pesticidas à base de nano partículas).

Embora a forma preventiva mais eficaz, seja tão simples quanto assegurar que todos os procedimentos são correctos e seguros de se realizar, bem antes de os realizar em massa. Certo é que ainda existem poucas formas de detectar, medir a toxicologia das nano partículas nos humanos como no meio ambiente, para poder prevenir riscos maiores.

Outra forma preventiva, será ter uma ventilação funcional e de acordo com a Higiene e Segurança do Trabalho, por sua vez um controlo maior por parte dos técnicos de Higiene e Segurança do Trabalho, juntamente com os engenheiros de controlo ou engenheiros especializados na área de nano partículas, para minimizar possíveis danos.

A nível de pele e possíveis causas de doenças pulmonares, convém ter equipamentos protectores, como luvas feitas à base de nano partículas, ou luvas revestidas, onde haja menor risco de contacto directo com a pele, óculos protectores, em caso de se estar directamente exposto com a face, uma farda que proteja o corpo devidamente, eventuais máscaras para proteger as narinas e boca, de eventuais substâncias que possam fluir na atmosfera.

4. Conclusão

Tendo em consideração, que este tema, é algo que está num processo crescente, foi importante procurar entender melhor o tema, as questões colocadas neste trabalho, como saber o que realmente são nano partículas, bem como se pode tentar prevenir os seus malefícios.

Olhando um pouco para trás, foi algo que tomei conhecimento, numa época onde os jogos virtuais, gostavam de andar com teorias e fórmulas à frente, para atrair pessoas entusiastas da realidade virtual, como da ficção científica e futurística, sendo o 'Crysis', um dos jogos primórdios que começou a mencionar fatos feitos de nano partículas, entre outros pontos, e passado alguns anos, realmente já ser possível existir fatos de nano partículas, é algo deveras fascinante.

Hoje em dia, apesar das prevenções que devem ser tomadas e as cautelas que devem ser feitas e estudadas quanto ao uso de nano partículas, acabam por ser partículas, que formam tecidos, compostos, dando o exemplo da nanotecnologia, que cada vez mais e com maior primor, ajudam pessoas incapacitadas a ter uma segunda chance, seja num membro que perderam, seja para terem o que por ventura, nem tiveram durante uma vida inteira, logo então, este livro espero que vos seja útil a vós leitores.

Despeço-me até a um próximo livro!

Outros livros do autor:

- Poesias de Luís (Volume I)
- Poetry of Luís (Volume II)
- Poesias de Luís (Volume III)
- Factores Críticos de Sucesso
- Another Way of Watching the Romance of the Three Kingdoms
- There Is Something About Leadership: Be a Leader

Informações do autor:

Website – www.luisjcosta.com

Facebook Author Page -

https://www.facebook.com/LCostaAutor

Referências Bibliográficas & Netgrafia

Brun, E. [2009], *Expert forecast on emerging chemical risks related to occupational safety and health*. European Agency for Safety and Health at Work, 2009.

Ribeiro, T. [2014], *Materiais Híbridos Fluorescentes*. CQFM – Centro de Química- Física Molecular e IN – Institute of nanoscience and Nanotechnology, Universidade de Lisboa, 2014.

Olhar Nano [2016], *Estabilização de Nanopartículas: O que é e qual a sua finalidade?*
– Maio 2016, Acedido em 10 de Novembro de 2016,
http://www.olharnano.com/artigos/4001/32001/Estabiliza%C3%A7%C3%A3o-de-nanopart%C3%ADculas:-o-que-%C3%A9-e-qual-sua-finalidade

Conversor de Unidades [2016], *Conversor de Unidades por comprimento* – Novembro 2016, Acedido em 10 de Novembro de 2016, http://www.converter-unidades.info/conversor-de-unidades.php?tipo=comprimento

Dicionário Priberam [2016], *Nanopartícula* –
Novembro 2016, Acedido em 10 de Novembro de
2016, www.priberam.pt/dlpo/nanopartícula

Wikipedia [2016], *Nanopartícula* – Novembro 2016,
Acedido em 10 de Novembro de 2016,
https://pt.wikipedia.org/wiki/Nanopart%C3%ADcul
a

RTP [2016], *Nano partículas encontradas no cérebro
humano podem causar Alzheimer*, Agência Lusa –
Setembro 2016, Acedido em 10 de Novembro de
2016, http://www.rtp.pt/noticias/mundo/nano-
particulas-encontradas-no-cerebro-humano-
podem-causar-alzheimer_n945400

RTP [2014], *Portugueses desenvolvem fato de proteção para
pesticidas à base de nanopartículas*, Agência Lusa –
Fevereiro 2014, Acedido em 10 de Novembro de 2016,
http://www.rtp.pt/noticias/economia/portugueses-
desenvolvem-fato-de-protecao-para- pesticidas-a-base-
de-nanoparticulas_n716632

Anexos

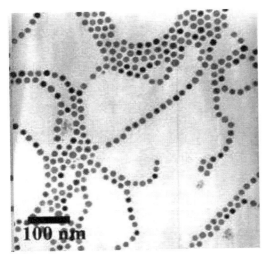

*Figura 3 - Nano partículas de Cobalto, créditos
NIST (EUA)*

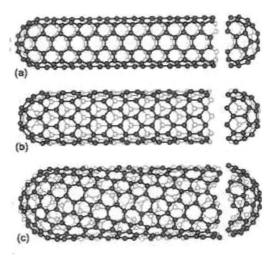

*Figura 4 - Diferentes tipos de nanotubos de carbono. Créditos - University
of Bristol*

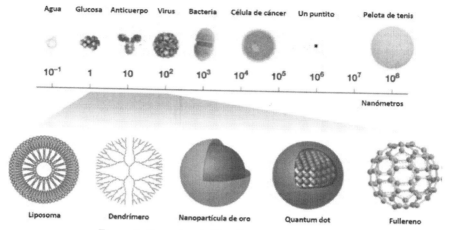

Figura 5- Exemplos de NanoParticulas

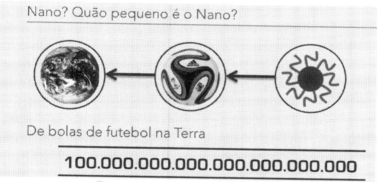

Figura 6 - Quão Pequeno é "Nano"

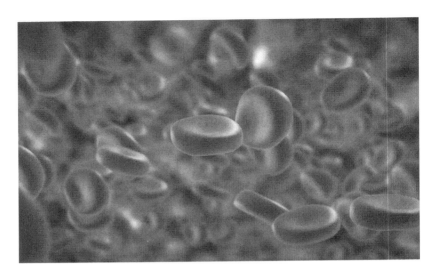

Figura 7 - As Nano Partículas podem afectar directamente no sangue

Pequenos excertos retirados da notícia/artigo da RTP:

"Estes resultados sugerem que as nano partículas de magnetita presentes no ambiente podem penetrar no cérebro humano, onde podem representar um risco para a saúde", escrevem os autores do estudo, citados pela agência AFP.

"Estas partículas parecem-se com as nano esferas de magnetita que encontramos frequentemente nas partículas em suspensão no ar em meio urbano"

"Não sabemos o suficiente para estabelecer se esta fonte externa de magnetita provocada pela poluição do ar pode ser um factor desta doença", disse no entanto Joanna Collingwood, da Universidade de Warwick.

"Não penso que possamos dizer neste momento se isso causa a doença de Alzheimer, mas é uma fonte de preocupação porque as partículas de magnetita têm sido associadas a outros problemas de saúde, como doenças cardiovasculares e pulmonares", disse por seu lado Peter Dobson, do King`s College de Londres.

13278087R00020

Printed in Germany
by Amazon Distribution
GmbH, Leipzig

THE ILLUSTRATED BOOK OF ODD LITTLE SAYINGS

Everyday Phrases and Their Origins

SALLY MOONEY

Contents

3

Preface

If you've ever wondered about the odd little sayings that people throw into everyday conversation, you are not alone. For example, sayings like, "let's make a toast", "she's opened up a can of worms with that" or "he got out of bed on the wrong side", are all odd things to say when you consider the words in a literal sense. Sayings like these are known also as idioms. An idiom is a group of words with a figurative, non-literal meaning, which can't usually be deciphered by looking at the words alone.

Whilst there are literally thousands of sayings and phrases in the English language, today we find that many are seldom used and some are simply not understood at all. Many sayings date back hundreds of years and we can learn a lot about history, local culture and customs from them, making it a real shame if they were to die out. It appears that many people would agree with this sentiment.

In a recent survey conducted by Prospectus Global in 2022, seventy-three per cent of the respondents felt that it was a great shame when sayings died out. The survey was conducted across two thousand adults living in Britain, aged between eighteen and fifty. They were asked about a number of sayings and phrases to see which ones they used and understood. As many as sixty-four per cent of the respondents had never used or heard of the saying, "a stitch in time saves nine". I was quite surprised at this as it's a saying I know all too well, having been raised in a thrifty household. Needless to say, you will discover its meaning and origin later in this book.

Many of the sayings familiar to me, I originally heard from my mother, who still uses them today at the age of eighty-six. My mother grew up in Vienna, Austria and moved to England in her early twenties. At that time, her spoken English was limited, so I was curious as to how she knew so many of these odd little sayings when English wasn't her mother tongue. When I recently asked her about this, she explained that it was often much easier to convey what she wanted to say with a saying as opposed to trying to find the correct English words to get the same message across.

It made me think that years ago, education was not what it is today. Many people didn't learn to read and write and they wouldn't have had a large vocabulary. It would have been important to share messages of advice, warnings and words of wisdom quickly and easily, so maybe that is why so many sayings came about. They are short and sweet and often have a rhyming nature, making them a simple, fun and memorable way to get a message across.

So, "let's not beat around the bush anymore" and let me tell you about this book. Having received such enthusiasm for my first book, "The Illustrated Book of Funny Old Sayings", I was encouraged to write another. So here we have "The Illustrated Book of Odd Little Sayings" which is full of even more everyday phrases and their origins. Whilst the origins for some are unequivocal, the origins for others are questionable. In these instances, I have chosen to share what I believe to be the most likely.

Each saying is matched with a unique and playful illustration, painted by the talented, Ecaterina Leascenco. She has the extraordinary ability to paint the pictures in my head, which is no easy task, I'm sure! The illustrations are often a literal interpretation of the saying, so it can be fun to see if you can guess the name of the saying from just looking at the picture alone.

At the back of this book, you will see instructions on how to get our FREE BONUS "Sayings Game" which you can play with your family and friends. If you previously bought our first book, "The Illustrated Book of Funny Old Sayings", you may have received the "Sayings Game" which was sent as a thank you gift for purchasing it. The game involves taking a card from the pack and seeing if you can guess the name of the saying from looking at the picture. So if you already have this game, you can add these new cards to the original pack. The game can easily be played with either one or both sets of cards.

Remember, "Life is more fun if you play games" - Roald Dahl

Enjoy!

Barking up the wrong tree

We will often say that someone is barking up the wrong tree if they are making a false assumption about someone or something, or are clearly going down the wrong track with regards to fixing a problem.

The origin of this phrase relates to hunting dogs and was being used figuratively back in the 1800's. Dogs have been used to chase and track down animals for many years due to their very strong sense of smell. However, anyone who knows anything about dogs, will know that they can easily get distracted.

If a dog happened to spot a different animal it may well give chase to that instead. And, if that animal was able to escape by climbing a tree, it would be wise to do so as dogs are not so great at climbing trees. The dog would remain at the bottom and bark instead, indicating to the hunter that the animal was up there, albeit the wrong animal. It's not surprising then that this phrase came about, as the dog would quite literally be barking up the wrong tree.

You can lead a horse to water but you can't make it drink

This frequently used phrase is so true! It means whilst you can give someone the opportunity to do something, you cannot force them to do it if they don't want to. People can be very strong minded, just like horses and won't do things that they don't want to do.

Many proverbs can give richness to language and can define a culture. It is thought that this one in particular encapsulates the English people's mindset better than any other saying. It is in fact one of the oldest English proverbs that is still in regular use today, being recorded as early as 1175 in the Old English Homilies

Shut your face

I remember my brothers saying this to each other when growing up and arguing about something. It is of course a rather rude way to tell someone to be quiet or to shut up.

The phrase "shut up" meaning to conclude or bring to a close was found in the 16th century. Just a century later, the same phrase was used meaning to be quiet, to literally shut up one's mouth.

Whilst it is unclear as to the actual origin of "shut your face", one theory suggests it relates to knights in shining armour that wore full face plates. It's easy to comprehend that once the face plate was pulled down covering the face or shutting off the face, speech would have effectively been limited.

Break the ice

If you have worked or are working in a business environment, it is likely that you are very familiar with this saying. When we break the ice, we are taking the initiative to break down the formalities and build rapport with a person or a group of people prior to getting down to business.

Long before the days of trains and cars, port cities that thrived on trade suffered during the winter months because the rivers froze, preventing commercial ships from entering the city. So smaller ships, known as "icebreakers" would rescue the large icebound ships by breaking the ice and creating a path for them to follow, enabling trade to continue. Before any type of business arrangement today, it is customary to "break the ice" before beginning a meeting, presentation or project.

Keep your shirt on

In a heated situation, you may well tell someone to keep their shirt on, meaning stay calm and don't lose your temper.

Shirts in the earlier days were rather expensive and could be quite restrictive. So, when a man was thinking about fighting someone, he would take off his shirt to both prevent it from being ripped and to allow full upper body movement. Those people who were not interested in fighting or seeing a fight take place, would advise the angry person to keep their shirt on, quite literally!

Paint the town red

If you're someone who likes to party, then it's quite likely that you have heard this said. "Let's go out and paint the town red" is an old English idiom which pretty much means, let's go out and have a wild night, with lots to drink and have heaps of fun.

In 1837, the Marquis of Waterford led a group of friends on a night of drinking through the English town of Melton Mowbray. The group of friends caused rather a lot of damage that night, including painting the tollgate, several homes and a swan statue in bright red paint. Hence the term "painting the town red" refers to a wild night out and has been in use ever since.

Stuck between a rock and a hard place

You're stuck between a rock and hard place if you're in a dilemma, having to choose between two equally difficult and undesirable situations.

This phrase actually originated in America in the early part of the twentieth century and was used more frequently during the Great Depression of the 1930's when many people were faced with hardship and difficult choices.

The first known citation of this phrase was recorded in 1921, following the 1907 Bankers' Panic and the financial crisis of 1917 which resulted in a huge dispute between copper miners and the mining companies in Bisbee, Arizona. Some of the workers organised themselves into labour unions and approached management with a list of demands for better pay and safer conditions. These demands were refused and it is said that over a thousand striking miners, plus others were kidnapped and illegally deported to New Mexico. Given the choice between harsh and underpaid work at the rock-face, versus unemployment and poverty which is equally a hard place to be in, one can surmise that this is the source of the phrase.

Fish out of water

We say someone is like a fish out of water when they are out of their comfort zone and they are in a completely unsuitable or unnatural environment or situation.

The natural habitat of a fish is in the water and it's the place where it is most comfortable. If you remove a fish from that environment and drop it onto land, it flops and wiggles around as it desperately seeks water and tries to find its way back home.

At some point, people must have noticed how awkward a fish looks after being taken out of the water and this became a metaphor for people who look to be out of their comfort zone.

Showing your true colours

If you show your true colours, then you are revealing your true nature and showing your real personality as opposed to how you have been perceived. You may have been behaving in a certain way to deliberately or deceptively mislead.

This phrase has a nautical origin, dating back to the 1700's and refers to the colour of the flag which every ship was required to fly at sea. Pirates used to deceive other ships by sailing under false flags so that they would not create suspicion. When other ships approached thinking they were safe, they became easy targets for an attack. It was only after the attack that the pirates would show their true flag.

Caught red handed

We might say that someone has been "caught red handed" if they have been caught in the act of committing a crime or doing something wrong. It can be used to describe someone committing a serious crime, like robbing a shop and being caught leaving with the stolen goods in their possession, or it can be used to describe a small child being caught eating sweets when they were specifically told not to.

Today of course, this idiom has nothing to do with red hands, but like many idioms the term was first used in a fairly literal sense. The phrase was originally used in Scotland during the 15th century. People were described as "red hand" or "redhand" when caught literally with blood on their hands after committing a murder, or from poaching an animal.

Put your thinking cap on

The phrase "put your thinking cap on" means take time to consider and think about a difficult or important matter in order to come up with a solution.

A "thinking cap" was previously known by the name of a "considering cap". That term has gone entirely out of use now but was known since the early 17th century. Perhaps the most famous considering cap was the one described in "The history of little Miss Goody Two-shoes", an anonymous work published by John Newbery in 1765. The author describes a considering cap possessed by a Mrs Margery which was "almost as large as a Grenadier's, but of three equal sides". On the first of which was written, "I may be wrong"; on the second, "It is fifty to one but you are"; and the third, "I'll consider it". It seems strange, but people really did use thinking caps when considering difficult problems.

Pigs might fly

Well we all know that pigs can't fly and we would certainly be in shock if they did! This remark is often said in jest in response to the unlikeliness or the impossibility of an event happening. For example, my husband said that he would make a start on clearing out his wardrobe this week and I instantly responded with "and pigs might fly," as I knew he was highly unlikely to do it, being that it's a job he's been putting off for months.

The phrase has been used in various forms since the 1600's. The original version was "pigs fly with their tails forward", which was found in the 1616 edition of John Withals's English-Latin dictionary – A Shorte Dictionarie for Yonge Begynners. The entry reads "Pigs fly in the ayre with their tayles forward." This expression was used as a sarcastic rebuttal to an overly optimistic prediction, in much the same way as we use the shorter version "pigs might fly" today

More than you can shake a stick at

This is a humorous way of saying you have a lot of something, far more than you can count or need.

The origin of this saying is uncertain. One theory is simply that farmers controlled their sheep by shaking and pointing their staffs (crooks) at the animals to indicate where they should go. If the farmers had more sheep than they could control, then it seems plausible that "they had more than they could shake a stick at."

However, the first known citing of the phrase was in 1818 in the Lancaster Journal of Pennsylvania: "We have in Lancaster as many taverns as you can shake a stick at." The word "shake" is also a term for wood which has been cut into very small pieces, often used for cladding. Around the time this phrase was cited, "shakes" would have been the most common way of cladding a building's roof or walls, so the word "shake" would widely be understood in this context. It's hard to know, but it's likely that the phrase meant something similar to "more taverns than there are pieces you could split a log into."

A storm in a teacup

Another odd little idiom used to describe a situation or problem that has blown out of all proportion and may well have resulted in anger or rage completely disproportionate to the situation itself.

The basic sentiment of this phrase seems to have originated in 52 BC in the writings of Cicero, a Roman poet who refers to "stirring up billows in a ladle". Many cultures have versions of the phrase in their own languages. For example, the Netherlands version translates to "a storm in a glass of water" and the Hungarians, "a tempest in a potty". The first citing in English was in 1678, referring to "a storm in a cream bowl" and in 1830, there is reference to "a storm in a wash-hand basin". In 1825, the American rendition of "a tempest in a teapot" was recorded and then 13 years later, the UK version "a storm in a teacup". It seems that both "a tempest in a teapot" and "a storm in a teacup" both originated in Scotland.

Whilst there are many variations on a theme, clearly a storm in a small vessel such as a teapot or a cream bowl really wouldn't be worth getting upset about when compared to a storm in a vessel at sea.

In the limelight

Someone is said to be in the limelight if they are the centre of attention or in the public eye. It could be that they are being talked about a lot, interviewed or constantly photographed. We often refer to celebrities, actors and actresses as being in the limelight, so it's not surprising that this phrase originates back to theatres of old.

When calcium oxide (commonly known as lime) is heated, it produces a bright white light. In 1826, a Scottish engineer called Thomas Drummond first used this discovery to aid map reading in poor weather. Shortly afterwards, scientists developed his invention to produce other powerful lights, which were used as spotlights in theatres to focus attention on the main performer. The person standing in the limelight was of course the main focus of attention and so we have the origin of this saying.

Head over heels in love

This well-known saying is a great example of how language can communicate meaning even when it makes no literal sense at all. Let's face it, our head is normally over our heels. To be "head over heels in love" is to be madly in love, completely and utterly enamoured by the other person.

It is actually an extension of the phrase "head over heels" which means excited. Interestingly, the phrase originated in the 1300's as "heels over head", referring to the art of performing cartwheels and somersaults, literally being upside down with heels over head. It wasn't until the 1800's that the phrase "head over heels" was coined and gained its figurative meaning of excited. It seems likely that this came about as it would have been incredibly exciting for both those watching and performing the cartwheels and somersaults. Today the phrase most often used is "head over heels in love."

A stitch in time saves nine

An idiom providing words of wisdom and advice, meaning that it is better to solve a problem as early as possible, as it will save you time by not allowing it to become a bigger problem. Many believe that putting off doing something until later, creates more work in the long run.

The saying first appeared in print in 1732 in Thomas Fuller's collection of proverbs. Fuller recorded a large number of the early proverbs and believed that verses are easier to remember by heart and stick faster in the memory than prose. Ordinary people were much taken with the clinking of syllables, such that many proverbs were often formed as false rhymes.

As a child, I heard my mother use this saying often when mending our clothes. Being one of five children, there was a lot of mending to be done. I took the words literally and thought that it meant it was better to repair a small hole straight away, as it would save you nine stitches if you put it off and allowed the hole to get bigger. Although no one knows for sure who came up with this saying or what significance stitches or the number nine have, many people believe it was actually started by mothers tired of mending their children's clothing, just as I imagined as a young child. Why the number nine you may ask, maybe it's because it rhymes with time.

One card short of a deck

This is one of many derogatory phrases which is used to imply someone is either mentally, psychologically or intellectually deficient. The other similar phrase "not playing with a full deck" means the same.

The word "deck" here refers to a deck of playing cards. There is a popular story that the origin of this phrase dates back to the 1500's when playing cards was a popular form of entertainment. It is said that at this time a tax was levied against decks of cards. People would get around the tax by purchasing decks of 51 cards instead of 52 cards, thereby not playing with a full deck or one card short of a deck. This is in fact a false story which originally circulated in a viral email purporting to solve the murky origins of certain idioms. This is however one of many phrases that emerged in the United States during the 1980's to describe someone "missing something upstairs". Similar phrases are "not firing on all cylinders" and "two bricks shy of a load".

Snug as a bug in a rug

When it's freezing cold outside and you are indoors, possibly all wrapped up in a blanket, feeling very comfortable, warm and cosy, then you are said to be as "snug as a bug in rug".

This saying is thought to allude to a moth larva happily feeding inside a rolled-up carpet. It was first recorded in 1769 when included in a play staged by British actor Davide Garrick in celebration of Shakespeare: "If she has the mopus's (money), I'll have her, as snug as a bug in a rug".

It is hard to know whether this phrase was in common use at that time or whether it had been in use for many years prior to this. What we do know is that Shakespeare himself was responsible for coining many of the popular phrases we use today.

Spend a penny

I often used to hear this phrase when growing up in England and I'm sure I used to say it myself. It simply means you need to use the toilet.

The expression is derived from the fact that coin operated locks were installed on public toilets in the UK in the mid 1800's and it literally cost one penny to unlock them and use the toilet. These pay toilets were used mostly by women as public male urinals were free.

By the 1970's, it cost more than a penny to use the toilets and as such the use of this phrase declined. Today, the phrase is rarely used at all.

Open up a can of worms

Another odd little saying, the meaning of which has nothing to do with worms, I'm happy to say. One might say, "Oh dear, you've opened up a can of worms with that statement," meaning that you've opened up or revealed a whole new set of problems which could prove to be complicated or even scandalous. You may well have done this unexpectedly.

In the early 1800's tinned and preserved food was introduced and became very popular in many homes across Britain, so naturally people would be disgusted if they opened a can only to find it crawling with maggots and worms.

The design and quality of the tin can was improved over the years, and it was Peter Durand, an Englishman, who received the first patent form King George III for a tin-plated iron can used as a food container in 1810. Oddly enough, it was almost fifty years later when the can opener was invented.

Steal your thunder

When someone steals your thunder, they are taking credit for something that you should have been credited for.

The expression was coined in the early 1700's by the playwright and critic John Dennis. He first discovered the sound of thunder could be reproduced to great effect by pummelling large tin sheets backstage at the Drury Lane Theatre in London. At that time sound effects were virtually unheard of and his idea added to the drama and drew much attention. His play however did not attract much attention and was replaced by Macbeth in a matter of weeks. Shortly afterwards the embittered Dennis saw a performance of Macbeth and was furious to hear his thunder being reproduced without his permission.

Get out of bed on the wrong side

We often say someone has got out of bed on the wrong side if they are being grumpy or bad tempered during the day.

The phrase originated in the ancient Roman empire. The Romans had a superstition that the left side of things was evil. Interestingly, the Latin word for left is "sinister". It was thought that evil spirits lay on the left side during the night and if someone got out of bed on the left side, then those evil spirits would possess their body during the day, bringing them bad luck. People often used to have the left side of the bed pushed up against a wall to stop them getting out on that side. This might be something to think about if you've a tendency to be grumpy in the mornings.

A wolf in sheep's clothing

My elderly mother used this saying recently when describing a man who had appeared to be so kind and caring, only to discover that once he had gained her trust, he began stealing money from her bank accounts. "He is a wolf in sheep's clothing," she said.

"A wolf in sheep's clothing" is someone who hides malicious intent behind their friendly and kind appearance. This expression can be found in one of Aesop's fables, dating back 1,400 years. In one particular story, a wolf wraps himself up in sheep's fleece and sneaks into a paddock without being noticed by the shepherd. Once inside, he sets eyes on his dinner and immediately eats one of the lambs before his deception can be discovered.

The actual origin of this saying however can be found in the Bible: Matthew 7:15 says, "Beware of false prophets, which come to you in sheep's clothing, but inwardly they are ravening wolves."

Stir up a hornet's nest

A phrase used to describe someone who says or writes something which stirs up trouble or causes a commotion. It may well lead to people getting angry or annoyed. So today, if someone posted something controversial on social media which caused a stir, it would be appropriate to say, they've stirred up a hornet's nest with that comment.

A hornet is a large angry wasp which can sting repeatedly if disturbed. They often make their nests in a hollow tree and hope to be left alone. If we, for any reason, disturb it or poke it, we will likely attract an unwanted, angry response.

To make a toast

This is a very popular saying still used frequently today. Someone is likely to "propose a toast" at a celebratory gathering. It could be a gathering to celebrate a wedding, a birthday, a retirement, a new baby or any special occasion. When someone says they would like "to make a toast" or "propose a toast" it means, let's raise a glass and have a drink in somebody's honour. It is polite to take a sip of your drink at this point.

Oddly enough, this phrase is in fact related to toast. It dates back to the 15th and 16th centuries when in society households, a small piece of spiced toast would be added to a glass of wine to improve the flavour and filter the sediment. This was known as "toasted wine" and when drunk it was in honour of another person, usually a lady. The phrase "to drink a toasted wine" was used and when the quality of wine improved and we no longer needed to add this piece of toast to it, we continued "to make a toast" in someone's honour.

A wild goose chase

"A wild goose chase" is a hopeless pursuit of something that is difficult to find or obtain. It can be very frustrating and can often feel like a complete waste of time.

Back in the early 1500's the term "wild goose chase" was used to describe a type of horse race. In a wild goose chase horse race, the lead rider galloped across the open countryside in an erratic pattern. At different intervals, subsequent riders had to follow the exact pattern of the lead rider. Whilst the idea of geese flying in formation and following a leader comes to mind, the exact rules of the game are unknown.

The phrase "wild goose chase" was first written by William Shakespeare in 1595, in his play Romeo and Juliet; "Nay, if thy wits run the wild-goose chase, I have done, for thou hast more of the wild-goose in one of thy wits than, I am sure, I have in my whole five."

To spill the beans

"To spill the beans" means to disclose a secret or reveal something prematurely.

The origin of this saying dates back to the ancient Greek process of voting, where votes were cast by placing one of two different coloured beans in a vase in order to show their approval or disapproval for a candidate. Usually a white bean meant yes, and a black or brown bean meant no. Sometimes a voter would accidently knock over the vase, revealing all of the beans and allowing everyone to see the otherwise confidential votes.

Skeleton in your cupboard

If we say someone is believed to have a skeleton in their cupboard, it means they have a dark or shameful secret in their past which they would prefer to keep private.

The expression originated in the medical profession in Britain. Even though it was illegal to dissect dead bodies for the purposes of medical research up until an Act of Parliament was passed in 1832 permitting them to do so, some physicians did so regardless.

It is also said that after dissections became legal, grave robbers would dig up newly buried corpses and sell them to unscrupulous doctors in an underhand way. This practice was of course frowned upon and the skeletons literally had to be kept hidden away in locked cupboards.

As fit as a fiddle

Who doesn't want to be as fit as a fiddle? This is a well know saying used to describe a person or an animal that is healthy, lively and in good condition.

Back in the medieval days, the fittest person was thought to be the fiddler who danced and scampered around joyfully as they played their music throughout the crowds. The phrase at the time was "as fit as a fiddler" which made a lot more sense don't you think?

About Sally Mooney

Living in Sydney, Australia and now retired from the corporate world, Sally has plenty of time to pursue her many interests and hobbies. She has always enjoyed being creative, writing little stories and poems, so it is no surprise that she has since published five books.

Sally was brought up in the South of England and it was not unusual for her to hear funny old sayings pop out of people's mouths, which she recalls as being a little odd at the time. A number of years ago, she developed a fascination for these sayings and started to research their meanings and origins, hence the idea for an illustrated book of sayings came about.

Sally's first book, "The Illustrated Book of Funny Old Sayings" published in 2020, has been very popular, appearing on Amazon's best seller lists on a number of occasions. With the encouragement and help from her friend Sam Clarke, she has now published this new book in the series of books about everyday phrases and sayings.

If you like odd little sayings as much as we do, then you might like to follow us on Facebook.

https://www.facebook.com/funnyoldsayingsOnFB

Bonus – "Sayings Game"

Thank you so much for purchasing this book!
If you like this book, we would be most grateful if you could help us out by taking a few moments and leaving us an honest review on Amazon. Thank you so much.

As a FREE BONUS for purchasing this book, we would like to gift you a game to play with your family and friends. The game involves taking a card from the pack and guessing what the saying is from the picture. We have had a lot of fun playing this ourselves.

Simply visit this link below and we will email you a pdf of all of the illustrations in the book, together with instructions on how to play the game.

https://www.sci-pty-ltd.com/bonusgame2

If you enjoyed this book, check out our other book in the series:

The Illustrated Book of Funny Old Sayings can be purchased from Amazon

https://www.amazon.com/Illustrated-Book-Funny-Old-Sayings/dp/B086Y397QV

Printed in Great Britain
by Amazon

33981463R00041